SOCIAL PSYCHOLOGY IN EVERYDAY LIFE

UNDERSTANDING HUMAN CONNECTIONS

DR. MINAKSHI BANSAL

This book is dedicated to all who believe in the power of human connections—those who strive to understand, improve, and cherish the relationships that shape our lives. To educators, students, professionals, and everyday individuals who recognize that our social interactions are the foundation of our personal growth and collective success. Your dedication to fostering deeper understanding and empathy in an ever-changing world is both essential and inspiring.

♡♡♡

Contents

Contents

ONE

FOUNDATIONS OF SOCIAL CONNECTIONS: EXPLORING THE BASICS

Human beings are inherently social creatures. From the moment we are born, we are engaged in a complex dance of interactions that not only define our individual experiences but also shape our identities within the wider community. Let's understand the foundational aspects of social connections, exploring the basic principles that govern our interactions and examining how these bonds influence both individuals and groups.

At the core of social psychology is the understanding that our thoughts, feelings, and behaviours are profoundly influenced by the actual, imagined, or implied presence of others. This concept, first introduced by social psychologist Floyd Allport in the 1920s, serves as a cornerstone for understanding the depth and breadth of human connections. It suggests that our perceptions of ourselves and the world around us are not solely products of our minds but are also shaped by our social interactions and the contexts in which they occur.

One of the most basic forms of human connection is attachment. Attachment theory, developed by John Bowlby and Mary Ainsworth, posits that the bonds formed between a child and their primary caregivers can influence social relationships throughout the individual's life. Secure attachment in infancy leads to a greater ability to form stable relationships in adulthood, whereas insecure attachment can result in relational difficulties. This theory highlights the importance of early interactions and their long-lasting effects on personal development.

Communication is another fundamental aspect of building and maintaining social connections. It is not merely the exchange of information but also the primary means through which relationships are initiated, developed, and sustained. Effective communication involves verbal and non-verbal cues that convey empathy, understanding, and respect. These cues are vital in developing trust and rapport, which are essential for deepening social bonds.

Social identity theory further explores how individuals perceive themselves within their social contexts. Developed by Henri Tajfel and John Turner, this theory describes how the groups to which we belong, such as our family, community, or nationality, play a critical role in shaping our identity. This group identity can influence our behaviors in profound ways, often leading us to act in accordance with group norms and expectations even when they conflict with our personal beliefs.

Another important aspect of social connections is the concept of social influence, which includes behaviors such as conformity, compliance, and obedience. These behaviors demonstrate how individuals' thoughts, feelings, and actions are often swayed by others, particularly in group settings or when under the authority of a perceived leader. The famous experiments by Solomon Asch on conformity and by Stanley Milgram on obedience starkly illustrate the power of social influence, showing how strong the pressure can be to align with group norms or authority figures.

Social facilitation, introduced by Norman Triplett, provides insights into how the presence of others can enhance or impair performance. This phenomenon indicates that performing a task in front of others, particularly a well-rehearsed task, can lead to enhanced performance due to increased arousal. Conversely, the presence of others can also lead to performance anxiety or distraction, which can impair the execution of less familiar tasks.

Beyond interpersonal relationships, social connections also have broader societal implications. For instance, the development of social capital—the networks of relationships among people who live and work in a particular society—enables societies to function more efficiently. High levels of social capital are associated with numerous positive outcomes, including improved mental health, reduced crime rates, and increased educational achievement. These benefits underscore the importance of fostering strong, healthy social connections within communities.

Furthermore, technology has dramatically transformed the landscape of social interactions in modern times. The rise of social media platforms has revolutionized how people connect, interact, and share information. While these platforms can help maintain and strengthen social bonds, particularly across long distances, they also present challenges such as the risk of isolation, cyberbullying, and the spread of misinformation.

Understanding the foundations of social connections is essential for grasping the complex web of interactions that define human life. From the psychological theories that explain our attachment styles and social behaviors to the societal impacts of our interconnectedness, it is clear that the fabric of human relationships is woven from many diverse threads. As we continue to explore and understand these fundamental aspects, we enrich our ability to navigate our social world more effectively, enhancing both individual and collective well-being. This exploration not only deepens our knowledge of social psychology but also empowers us to create a more connected and harmonious society.

ϷϷϷ

"Social media bridges vast distances and cultures, creating a tapestry of shared experiences and insights. Yet, it demands a careful balance between connection and isolation, engagement and overwhelm."

ϼϼϼ

TWO

THE SCIENCE OF FIRST IMPRESSIONS: WHY THEY MATTER

First impressions are pivotal moments that often set the tone for all the ensuing relationships and interactions one might have. From a job interview to a casual social gathering, the initial impression can dictate how others perceive and interact with us. Understanding the science behind first impressions and why they hold such weight can help us navigate social interactions more effectively.

Research in social psychology suggests that first impressions are formed almost instantaneously—within mere seconds of meeting someone. This rapid formation of judgment, according to psychologists, arises from our evolutionary need to quickly assess a potential threat or ally. Malcolm Gladwell, in his book "Blink," suggests that our ability to gauge what others are thinking or feeling within the first few seconds is an adaptive human trait.

The elements that contribute to first impressions are manifold and include factors like appearance, body language, demeanor, voice tone, and even seemingly minor details like clothing choice or personal hygiene. For instance, studies have shown that people tend to associate physical attractiveness with positive qualities such as intelligence and kindness. This phenomenon, known as the "halo effect," illustrates how one favorable trait can influence people to assume other positive traits, regardless of whether they are present.

Body language also plays a crucial role in shaping first impressions. Non-verbal cues such as eye contact, posture, and facial expressions can convey confidence, openness, and friendliness, or their opposites—making them critical in the initial moments of interaction. Psychologist Amy Cuddy has emphasized the importance of body language in her research, which shows that adopting power poses can not only change how others perceive us but also how we see ourselves, boosting feelings of confidence.

Voice tone and speech patterns are equally impactful. Research indicates that a clear, well-modulated voice conveys intelligence and thoughtfulness, whereas a soft, mumbling voice might project uncertainty or lack of confidence. Similarly, the pace of speech can influence perceptions; speaking too quickly may suggest nervousness, while speaking too slowly might imply a lack of enthusiasm or interest.

The context in which a meeting occurs can also affect first impressions. Environmental factors such as the setting of the interaction, the mood of the participants, and even the time of day can influence how the interaction unfolds and is perceived by those involved. Social psychologists assert that our mental states and the environment can color our interpretation of social cues, further influencing our judgments.

Despite their rapid formation and sometimes baseless assumptions, first impressions are incredibly sticky and can be difficult to alter once formed. This resistance to change is due to the cognitive bias known as "confirmation bias," where people tend to seek out information that confirms their initial perceptions and overlook information that contradicts it. Consequently, a bad first impression can lead to a negative spiral where a person's actions are interpreted in a way that consistently reinforces the initial judgment.

Given the importance and enduring nature of first impressions, it is crucial to be mindful of how we present ourselves in new interactions. This doesn't mean altering one's personality but being aware of the non-verbal cues we emit and how these might be perceived. It also involves being attentive to others, providing them with a fair chance to express themselves without the cloud of our biases.

Moreover, understanding the dynamics of first impressions can enhance our empathy towards others. Recognizing that everyone may be dealing with different pressures and that they too are often judged by their first impression can lead to more compassionate interactions. It encourages a more conscious engagement with new acquaintances, where we actively decide to give them the benefit of the doubt and a chance to reveal their true selves over time.

The science of first impressions is a fascinating study of human interaction and psychology. It reveals how quickly we form judgments and how lasting those impressions can be, influencing our relationships and interactions. By understanding and mastering the elements that contribute to favorable first impressions, we can improve our social interactions and develop more meaningful relationships, both personally and professionally. Moreover, by approaching first impressions with awareness and empathy, we create a more understanding and connected social environment.

ᗰᗰᗰ

"In the dynamics of workplace behavior, collaboration and competition are two sides of the same coin. While competition drives excellence and innovation, collaboration ensures that this excellence is channeled towards collective success."

ppp

THREE

FORMATION OF FRIENDSHIPS: UNDERSTANDING ATTRACTION

Friendship is one of the most fundamental and valued aspects of human life, providing companionship, support, and a sense of belonging. The process of forming friendships involves a complex interplay of psychological dynamics, and central to this process is the concept of attraction. Attraction in friendships goes beyond the physical; it encompasses a range of factors including psychological compatibility, shared interests, and mutual respect and understanding.

The initial stage in the formation of any friendship is the mutual recognition of one or more attributes that draw two individuals together. These attributes can be as simple as common hobbies or as complex as shared values and worldviews. Psychologists have found that similarity is a key factor in attraction. This is explained by the 'similarity-attraction hypothesis,' which suggests that people are drawn to others who are like them, whether in terms of personality traits, background, or life goals. Similarity provides a basis for connection, making interactions more predictable and comfortable, thus facilitating deeper engagement and understanding.

Another significant factor in friendship attraction is proximity. According to the 'proximity principle,' people are more likely to become friends with individuals who are physically or situationally close to them. This could include neighbors, colleagues, or classmates. Proximity increases the likelihood of repeated interactions, which can lead to increased familiarity and comfort, laying the groundwork for friendship. This principle is well-documented in research, including studies that show higher rates of friendship formation among people who live near each other or attend the same classes.

Complementarity also plays a role in forming friendships. While similarity brings people together, complementarity can enhance the bond by balancing relationships through the strengths of one party complementing the weaknesses of the other. For instance, in a friendship, one person may be more extroverted and take the lead in social settings, helping a more introverted friend feel more comfortable. This balance can create a dynamic where both individuals feel they benefit from the relationship, enhancing their mutual attraction.

Interpersonal attraction in friendships is also significantly influenced by the reciprocal nature of liking. People tend to like others who like them in return. This reciprocal liking has a reinforcing effect on attraction, as knowing someone appreciates and values our company makes us feel good and more inclined to invest in that relationship. The effect of reciprocal liking is powerful in early interactions and can set a positive tone for the relationship's development.

Trust and emotional safety are critical in the formation of close friendships. Building trust involves consistent behavior over time, showing reliability, integrity, and emotional openness. When people feel they can share their thoughts and feelings without fear of judgment or rejection, emotional bonds deepen. This emotional safety allows friends to be vulnerable with each other, which is essential for developing intimacy and a lasting connection.

Moreover, the role of self-disclosure cannot be overstated in the context of forming friendships. Self-disclosure involves sharing personal information with another person, which contributes to the development of trust and intimacy. As friends share more about their lives, their challenges, and their dreams, they build a unique private world that further cements their bond. The gradual deepening of disclosure helps maintain the friendship's momentum, ensuring that it evolves and adapts over time.

Interestingly, modern technology has transformed the way friendships are formed and maintained. Social media and online platforms allow people to meet and interact regardless of physical barriers. Online friendships can develop around shared interests or experiences without the immediate need for physical proximity. However, the principles of attraction, including similarity and reciprocal liking, remain pivotal in these digital interactions.

The formation of friendships is a dynamic and multifaceted process driven by various factors, including similarity, proximity, complementarity, reciprocal liking, trust, and self-disclosure. Understanding these factors can help individuals navigate their social worlds more effectively, leading to the development of meaningful and enduring friendships. Friendships enrich our lives, providing emotional support and enhancing our personal growth, and understanding the underlying dynamics of attraction can help us foster deeper and more fulfilling relationships.

ﬁﬁﬁ

"Understanding cultural differences is more than an academic skill; it's a daily reality for millions navigating our globalized society. Embracing these differences enriches our personal and professional lives, creating a more inclusive and dynamic community."

❦❦❦

FOUR

The Psychology of Romantic Relationships: Love and Beyond

Romantic relationships are among the most profound of human connections, characterized not just by love, but also by companionship, conflict, and growth. The psychology behind these relationships is complex, influenced by various factors that affect how they begin, develop, and sometimes end.

Love, at its core, is a powerful emotion that has been the subject of much psychological research. Psychologists have identified several types of love, including passionate love and companionate love. Passionate love is marked by intense emotions, physical attraction, and anxiety about the relationship.

It is the kind of love often depicted in movies and literature, characterized by a deep absorption in another person. Companionate love, on the other hand, is defined by deep affection and commitment. It is less intense but more stable and grows over time, based on mutual respect, shared values, and enduring bonds.

The initial stages of a romantic relationship are often fueled by passionate love, which is why new relationships can feel so exhilarating and all-consuming. This stage is driven by biological processes, such as the release of hormones like dopamine and oxytocin, which enhance mood and create feelings of euphoria. However, for a relationship to endure long-term, it typically transitions into companionate love, which is necessary for developing a stable, lasting partnership.

Attachment theory, initially developed to describe the bonds between infants and caregivers, is also a useful framework for understanding romantic relationships. Adults display different attachment styles based on their early experiences with caregivers, and these styles can profoundly affect how they approach romantic relationships.

Secure attachment styles are associated with healthy, stable relationships, while insecure attachment styles, such as anxious or avoidant attachment, can lead to more conflict and dissatisfaction.

Communication is another crucial aspect of romantic relationships. Effective communication helps partners to express their needs, resolve conflicts, and share their feelings in a constructive manner. Poor communication can lead to misunderstandings and resentment, which are common sources of relationship strife. Active listening, empathy, and the ability to express oneself clearly are essential skills that foster good communication in relationships.

Conflict is inevitable in any relationship, but the way it is managed can determine the health and longevity of a partnership. Psychologists John Gottman and Robert Levenson studied the nature of conflict in relationships and identified four behaviors—criticism, contempt, defensiveness, and stonewalling—that are particularly destructive, termed "the Four Horsemen of the Apocalypse." Couples who learn to manage conflict constructively, without resorting to these behaviors, are more likely to sustain healthy relationships.

Trust and commitment are the bedrock of any lasting romantic relationship. Trust allows partners to feel secure, knowing their vulnerabilities will not be exploited. Commitment involves choosing to stay with a partner despite the inevitable ups and downs of life. These elements are fostered through actions that build partnership and through navigating life's challenges together, reinforcing the bond between partners.

Personal growth and mutual support are also vital components of a successful romantic relationship. Healthy relationships encourage individual partners to grow and achieve their potential. This can include supporting each other's career goals, personal interests, and spiritual growth. When both partners grow individually, the relationship can evolve and continue to be fulfilling.

Furthermore, the impact of societal and cultural factors cannot be underestimated. Cultural norms and societal expectations can influence the dynamics of romantic relationships, including the roles partners are expected to play and the way conflicts are resolved. Understanding these external influences can help couples navigate their relationship more effectively.

The psychology of romantic relationships encompasses a wide range of dynamics, from the initial spark of attraction to the deep commitment of long-term partnership. Understanding these psychological aspects can help individuals build stronger, more fulfilling relationships.

Love is more than just an emotion; it is a complex interplay of biology, personality, communication, and growth—all of which come together to form the foundation of romantic partnerships. Through this understanding, couples can foster a love that is not only passionate but also compassionate and enduring.

ppp

"Technology has not just changed how we communicate; it has redefined our very understanding of community. The digital realm offers both a new frontier for connection and a new challenge for genuine social interaction."

❧❧❧

FIVE

FAMILY DYNAMICS: THE TIES THAT BIND

Family is often seen as the foundational social unit in societies worldwide, playing a crucial role in the psychological and emotional development of individuals. Family dynamics—the interrelated, emotional, and behavioural patterns within a family—affect each member and shape how they interact with the world. Understanding these dynamics can provide insights into the complexities of family relationships and the profound influence they have on individual lives.

The concept of family has evolved significantly over the years, but the core idea remains the same: a group of people connected by genetic ties, legal bindings, or emotional bonds who often live together and provide mutual support. Within this unit, various factors influence the dynamics, including parenting styles, sibling relationships, and the roles each family member adopts.

Parenting styles are among the most significant factors impacting family dynamics. Psychologists have identified several main styles of parenting: authoritative, authoritarian, permissive, and neglectful. Each style affects children differently. Authoritative parenting, which is both responsive and demanding, tends to produce children who are self-confident, self-regulated, and socially adept.

Authoritarian parenting, which is demanding but not responsive, often results in children who are obedient and proficient, but with lower self-esteem and increased anxiety. Permissive parents are responsive but not demanding, leading to children who may struggle with self-control and authority. Finally, neglectful parenting, being neither responsive nor demanding, can result in children who lack self-esteem and are less competent in social settings.

Sibling relationships also play a critical role in shaping family dynamics. These relationships are often the longest-lasting bonds within a family. Siblings can be supportive, competitive, or indifferent toward each other, and these interactions can affect their behaviour outside the family. The rivalry is common and can be constructive if it encourages siblings to excel and develop their skills. However, intense competition can also lead to resentment and conflict. The birth order of siblings has been studied extensively, with findings suggesting it can influence personality and behaviour.

For example, firstborns are often seen as leaders and might be more achievement-oriented, while younger siblings might be more open to taking risks.

Family roles are another aspect of family dynamics. In many families, members naturally take on specific roles such as the caretaker, the peacemaker, or the troublemaker. These roles can influence how individuals behave within the family and how they perceive themselves. While these roles can provide a sense of identity within the family, they can also be restrictive. People might feel pressured to conform to their roles, limiting their behaviour and possibly leading to conflict.

Communication within a family is crucial for healthy dynamics. Effective communication helps members feel understood and supported, and can resolve conflicts. In contrast, poor communication can lead to misunderstandings and resentment. Open, honest communication fosters stronger relationships and better mutual understanding.

Conflict is inevitable in any relationship, including those within families. Managing conflict constructively is essential for maintaining healthy family dynamics. Families that handle disagreements effectively use conflicts to address and solve underlying issues, which can strengthen relationships. Conversely, families that handle conflicts poorly might see long-term relationship damage.

Cultural factors significantly influence family dynamics. Different cultures have varying expectations about roles within the family, how decisions are made, and how openly members are allowed to express their emotions. These cultural expectations can affect how family dynamics are perceived and judged both within and outside the family unit.

The emotional bonds that families form—through shared experiences, mutual support, and love—are what make these dynamics so influential. These bonds can provide a buffer against the stresses of life and support individuals in times of need. However, they can also complicate relationships and create emotional entanglements.

Family dynamics are complex and varied, shaped by numerous factors including parenting styles, sibling relationships, family roles, communication patterns, and cultural backgrounds. These dynamics play a crucial role in the psychological development of individuals and influence their behaviour in broader social contexts.

By understanding these dynamics, individuals can better navigate their family relationships, leading to healthier interactions and improved well-being for all family members. Understanding and addressing family dynamics can help break cycles of negative behavior and foster environments where all members can thrive.

ᐳᐳᐳ

"Every social interaction is a dance of identity, where we continuously negotiate our personal and social selves. Our ability to navigate this complex interplay determines both our personal happiness and our effectiveness in collaborative environments."

ᗡᗡᗡ

SIX

THE INFLUENCE OF CULTURE: SHAPING OUR SOCIAL WORLD

Culture profoundly shapes our views, behaviors, and interactions within society. It is the invisible bond that connects people within a community, imparting shared values, traditions, and norms that dictate how individuals perceive themselves and others. Understanding the influence of culture is crucial in comprehensively grasping the dynamics of human relationships and social structures.

Culture encompasses the customs, arts, social institutions, and achievements of a particular nation, people, or other social group. It includes beliefs, laws, knowledge, arts, morals, and any other capabilities and habits acquired by humans as members of society. Through culture, individuals learn how to behave, react, and expect others to behave. This cultural learning starts from a young age within the family and community and continues throughout life as people interact with different cultural groups.

One of the primary ways culture influences individuals is through the establishment of norms, which are the unwritten rules that dictate acceptable behavior within a society. These norms cover a wide range of behaviors, from fundamental interactions like greeting rituals to more significant aspects such as moral judgments. For example, in some cultures, direct eye contact is considered respectful and indicative of honesty, while in others, it might be perceived as challenging or inappropriate.

Language is another crucial aspect of culture that shapes social interactions. It is not only a tool for communication but also a means for conveying a culture's values and priorities. The structure and vocabulary of a language can influence the way people think and perceive the world. The theory of linguistic relativity, for instance, suggests that the language we speak affects our worldview. Thus, multilingual individuals might experience and interpret the world differently depending on the language they are using at the time.

Cultural values also play a significant role in shaping behavior. These values affect how people define success, the importance of individual versus collective achievements, and how relationships are valued. For example, in individualistic cultures, such as the United States and many Western European countries, independence and self-reliance are highly valued. In contrast, in collectivist cultures, like those in many Asian and African countries, community and familial relationships hold more significance. These cultural values not only influence personal ambitions and life choices but also affect interpersonal dynamics and the structure of social networks.

Religion, as part of cultural influence, also shapes societal norms and individual behaviors. Religious beliefs provide a framework for understanding the world and dictate a set of behaviors that align with spiritual doctrines. These beliefs can influence various aspects of life, including dietary restrictions, clothing, and practices surrounding birth, marriage, and death. Religion can also play a role in community cohesion, providing a sense of belonging and a network of support.

Cultural rituals and ceremonies reinforce social bonds and transmit cultural values across generations. These rituals, whether they are daily practices like tea ceremonies in Japan or annual celebrations like Diwali in India, serve as constant reminders of a culture's values and a person's role within that cultural context. They also provide an opportunity for members of the culture to reaffirm their commitment to these collective values and strengthen community ties.

Furthermore, the globalized world has led to increased cultural exchanges and interactions, resulting in cultural diffusion and sometimes cultural clashes. As people from different cultural backgrounds interact, they influence each other and often create a new, hybrid culture. However, these interactions can also lead to misunderstandings if cultural norms and values are not communicated clearly or respected.

Culture is a powerful force that shapes every aspect of human life, from individual identity to social structures and interactions. It influences how we see the world, how we behave, and how we relate to others. By understanding the influence of culture, individuals can better navigate their social environments and foster more meaningful and respectful interactions. Acknowledging and appreciating cultural differences is essential in our increasingly interconnected world, as it promotes tolerance, mutual respect, and a deeper understanding of the vast tapestry of human life.

ᛒᛒᛒ

"Effective leadership in any group requires an understanding of the subtle social forces at play. It's about guiding without imposing, inspiring without demanding."

ᗷᗷᗷ

SEVEN

SOCIAL NORMS AND CONFORMITY: THE INVISIBLE RULES

Social norms are the unwritten rules of behaviour that are considered acceptable in a group or society. These norms guide daily behaviour and have a profound influence on our interactions within the social world. Conformity, the action of matching attitudes, beliefs, and behaviours to group norms, is a powerful force that can influence both individual and group behaviour significantly. Understanding how social norms and conformity shape our lives can help us navigate complex social environments more effectively.

Social norms originate from the need for order and predictability in society. They help individuals understand what is expected of them in various situations, reducing uncertainties and facilitating smooth social interactions. These norms can be as simple as dressing appropriately for a specific occasion or as significant as following laws and regulations. Norms vary widely across different cultures and settings, reflecting the values and priorities of the community.

Conformity to these norms is driven by several psychological processes. One of the most compelling reasons people conform is the desire for acceptance. Humans are inherently social creatures, and belonging to a group provides security, identity, and support. To maintain their status within a group, individuals often align their behaviours with the group norms. This alignment can be so strong that people sometimes conform to group behaviours even when they conflict with their personal beliefs, a phenomenon highlighted in Solomon Asch's famous conformity experiments in the 1950s.

Another reason for conformity is the need for information, particularly in ambiguous or unfamiliar situations. When uncertain, individuals often look to the behaviour of others as a guide, assuming that these behaviours are appropriate responses. This type of conformity is known as informational social influence and is a testament to the power of social norms as a source of guidance.

Social norms also play a critical role in maintaining order and promoting cooperation within societies. By setting expectations for behaviour, norms discourage disruptive behaviours and encourage actions that promote group welfare. For instance, norms around fairness and reciprocity are fundamental in various social contexts, from simple interactions like taking turns speaking to more complex societal structures like legal and economic systems.

However, the influence of social norms is not always positive. Excessive conformity can stifle individuality and creativity, leading to environments where people are afraid to express dissent or propose new ideas. It can also perpetuate social inequalities and injustices if the norms reflect the biases of the dominant group. For example, norms that discriminate based on race, gender, or sexuality can be deeply harmful, suppressing the rights and opportunities of certain groups.

Resisting harmful norms and promoting positive change often requires courageous individuals who are willing to challenge the status quo. Social change typically begins when individuals question existing norms and advocate for alternative practices that are more inclusive and just. Over time, with sustained effort and support, these new behaviours can become the norm, reshaping the social landscape.

Education plays a crucial role in understanding and addressing the impacts of social norms and conformity. By learning about these concepts, individuals can become more aware of how their behaviour is influenced by societal expectations and more capable of making informed choices about when to conform and when to resist.

Social norms and conformity are integral aspects of social life, providing structure and guidance for appropriate behaviour while also shaping the identity and actions of individuals within a society. While often beneficial, these invisible rules can also reinforce negative behaviours and inequalities. Awareness and critical examination of these norms are essential for individuals who wish to navigate their social environments effectively and ethically. Understanding the dynamics of social norms and conformity allows individuals to balance the benefits of social integration with the need for personal autonomy and social justice.

ᐅᐅᐅ

"Altruism isn't just a noble trait; it's a vital social mechanism that strengthens communities and fosters a culture of support and resilience."

♥♥♥

EIGHT

GROUP DYNAMICS: ROLES, CONFLICTS, AND COHESION

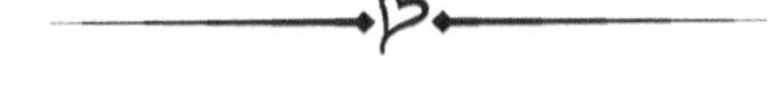

Group dynamics are essential elements that determine how a group functions, achieves its objectives, and maintains harmony or manages conflict. The interplay of roles, conflicts, and cohesion within a group can either facilitate its success or contribute to its challenges. Understanding these dynamics is crucial for anyone involved in managing teams, participating in groups, or studying social interactions.

Roles in Group Dynamics In any group, individuals assume various roles that contribute to the group's overall functioning. These roles can be formal, like a designated team leader or project manager, or informal, such as a mediator who emerges naturally within the group. Each role comes with expectations that can shape the group's dynamics and influence its effectiveness. Some roles support the group's task completion, while others focus on maintaining group harmony and managing relationships. For example, task-oriented roles might include initiators who propose new ideas, elaborators who build on those ideas, and completers who ensure tasks are finished. Relationship-oriented roles could be supporters who provide encouragement, harmonizers who resolve conflicts, or gatekeepers who manage communication flow.

Conflict in Group Dynamics Conflict is an inevitable aspect of group dynamics and can stem from a variety of sources, such as competition for resources, differences in goals, or personality clashes. Conflict isn't inherently negative; it can foster healthy debate, spur innovation, and lead to better solutions. However, when managed poorly, it can lead to frustration, decreased productivity, and a toxic environment. Effective conflict management involves recognizing the sources of conflict, understanding the different perspectives, and facilitating solutions that are acceptable to all parties involved. Techniques such as mediation, compromise, and consensus-building are often employed to manage conflicts constructively.

Cohesion in Group Dynamics Cohesion refers to the bonds that hold a group together and is critical for its long-term success. High levels of cohesion can lead to increased satisfaction among group members, greater cooperation, and improved performance. Cohesion is built through shared goals, mutual respect, and the development of strong interpersonal relationships among group members. Activities that foster teamwork and a sense of belonging can enhance cohesion. However, too much cohesion can also have drawbacks, such as resistance to change and groupthink, where the desire for harmony results in poor decision-making.

Balancing Roles, Conflicts, and Cohesion The key to successful group dynamics lies in balancing these elements effectively. Clear communication is essential in defining roles and responsibilities, which helps in minimizing misunderstandings and conflicts. Leaders play a pivotal role in this aspect by providing direction, facilitating open communication, and ensuring that all members feel valued and understood.

Leaders are also crucial in managing conflicts. They need to be adept at recognizing the signs of conflict early and addressing them in a way that is fair and respectful to all parties involved. This might involve direct interventions, fostering an environment where open dialogue is encouraged, or sometimes reallocating roles to better suit the group's needs and the individual's strengths.

Similarly, fostering cohesion requires a careful approach. While it's important to build a strong, unified team, it's equally important to encourage diversity of thought and opinion. Leaders can encourage this by celebrating differences, promoting inclusiveness, and ensuring that all members have opportunities to contribute.

Practical Applications In the workplace, understanding group dynamics can help in assembling teams that are effective, innovative, and harmonious. In educational settings, teachers and students can benefit from this understanding by creating learning environments that are cooperative and supportive. In personal relationships, insights into group dynamics can improve how families and friends interact and support each other.

Understanding and managing group dynamics effectively is critical for the success of any group. By appreciating the roles individuals play, managing conflicts wisely, and fostering a cohesive environment, groups can achieve their objectives while maintaining a positive and productive atmosphere. This balance is not always easy to achieve but is essential for the long-term effectiveness and satisfaction of group members. Through continuous effort and mindful management of these dynamics, groups can navigate the complexities of collaboration and achieve outstanding results.

PPP

"Prejudices in the mind can translate into barriers in society. Overcoming them requires not only individual introspection but also collective action towards more inclusive behaviors."

ᎮᎮᎮ

NINE

LEADERSHIP AND POWER IN GROUPS: NAVIGATING INFLUENCE

Leadership and power are central themes in the study of group dynamics, as they directly affect how groups are formed, function, and achieve their goals. Understanding how leadership styles and power structures influence group behaviour can provide valuable insights into the effective management of teams and organizations.

Leadership in Groups Leadership within a group is not merely about holding a position of authority; it involves guiding the group towards achieving its objectives while fostering a positive and productive environment. Effective leaders are those who can motivate and inspire group members, manage resources wisely, and navigate the complexities of group dynamics.

There are several key leadership styles, each with its own strengths and weaknesses:

Autocratic leadership involves clear, directive commands from the leader with little input from group members. This style can be effective in situations where quick decisions are necessary, but it may stifle creativity and reduce members' engagement.

Democratic leadership encourages group participation in decision-making processes, helping to increase investment and cooperation but possibly slowing down decision-making.

Transformational leadership focuses on inspiring and motivating team members to exceed their own expectations and those of the organization. Leaders who employ this style are often seen as charismatic and influential.

Servant leadership emphasizes the needs of the team and organization before those of the leader. Servant leaders often build strong loyalty and cooperation within their teams.

Each style impacts group dynamics differently and can be more or less effective depending on the group's context, objectives, and members' personalities.

Power in Groups Power within a group can arise from various sources and is not limited to the formally appointed leaders. Power dynamics can influence relationships within the group, affecting communication, decision-making, and the overall atmosphere.

The sources of power in a group typically include:

Legitimate power, derived from the official authority to make decisions.

Expert power, based on the knowledge and skills that a member brings to the group.

Referent power, stemming from a member's ability to attract others and build loyalty based on charisma or likeability.

Reward power, involving the capability to distribute rewards to other group members.

Coercive power, which is the ability to punish or control others.

Understanding these different types of power can help group members and leaders manage influence more effectively, ensuring that it is used constructively rather than destructively.

Navigating Leadership and Power Navigating leadership and power within a group requires awareness and careful management. Leaders must recognize their own influence, understand the dynamics at play, and strive to use their power to promote group cohesion and success. This involves:

Being transparent about decision-making processes.

Encouraging open communication and feedback from all group members.

Recognizing and utilizing the diverse skills and abilities of group members.

Managing conflicts constructively and fairly.

Fostering a culture of respect and mutual support.

Challenges in Leadership and Power Dynamics Groups often face challenges related to leadership and power, including power struggles, leadership transitions, and conflicts arising from misuse of power. These challenges can disrupt group cohesion and impede performance.

To effectively manage these challenges, leaders should focus on:

Developing a clear understanding of each member's expectations and concerns.

Facilitating training and development opportunities to prepare future leaders.

Establishing clear, equitable rules and procedures for the exercise of power and resolution of conflicts.

Regularly evaluating and adjusting leadership approaches to better meet the needs of the group.

Effective leadership and the wise use of power are critical for the success of any group. Leaders who are able to navigate these aspects skilfully can enhance group performance, foster a positive environment, and lead their teams towards achieving complex goals. By understanding the dynamics of leadership and power, leaders can ensure that they are using their influence constructively, promoting a culture of accountability, respect, and mutual success within the group. Through continuous learning and adaptation, leaders can not only guide their current groups but also prepare them for future challenges and opportunities.

ᐅᐅᐅ

"Virtual reality offers us a new way to face our fears and rehearse our strengths in a controlled environment, promising breakthroughs in both therapeutic settings and everyday life."

ᛞᛞᛞ

TEN
Persuasion and Attitude Change: The Art of Influence

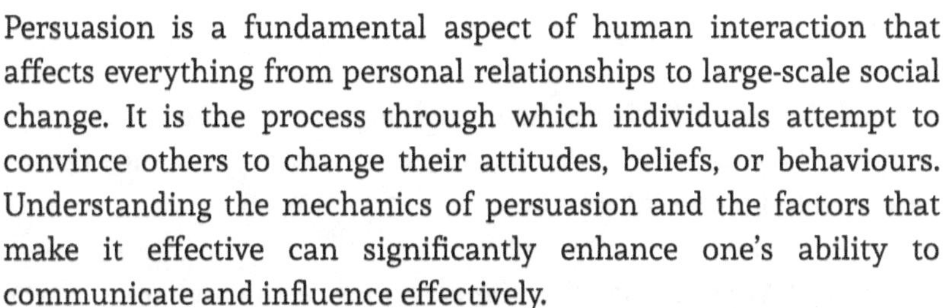

Persuasion is a fundamental aspect of human interaction that affects everything from personal relationships to large-scale social change. It is the process through which individuals attempt to convince others to change their attitudes, beliefs, or behaviours. Understanding the mechanics of persuasion and the factors that make it effective can significantly enhance one's ability to communicate and influence effectively.

The Foundations of Persuasion At its core, persuasion involves communication that is designed to influence the cognitive processes of another person. This can involve straightforward appeals to logic and reason, emotional appeals, or a combination of both. The key to effective persuasion lies in understanding the audience's pre-existing attitudes and beliefs, as well as the context in which the persuasion occurs.

Several psychological theories have been developed to explain how persuasion works. One of the most influential is the Elaboration Likelihood Model (ELM), proposed by Richard Petty and John Cacioppo. This model suggests that there are two primary pathways through which persuasion can occur: the central route and the peripheral route. The central route involves deep, thoughtful consideration of the arguments presented, which is most effective when the audience is motivated and able to think about the message. The peripheral route, on the other hand, involves less scrutiny and is influenced by external cues such as the attractiveness or credibility of the source or the emotional appeal of the message.

Key Elements of Persuasive Communication Effective persuasive communication typically involves several key elements:

Credibility: The persuader must be seen as trustworthy and knowledgeable. Credibility can be enhanced by demonstrating expertise, conveying honesty, and building a rapport with the audience.

Logical Argument: Using clear and logical arguments that are supported by data or evidence can help sway an audience that is receptive to factual information.

Emotional Appeal: Engaging the emotions of the audience can be a powerful tool in persuasion, especially when logical arguments alone are insufficient. Emotional appeals can include appeals to fear, happiness, sadness, or pride.

Audience Engagement: Understanding the audience's values, needs, and potential objections is crucial. Tailoring the message to meet these needs and engaging with the audience to make them feel heard and understood can significantly increase the effectiveness of persuasion.

Techniques for Enhancing Persuasion Several techniques can be employed to enhance the effectiveness of persuasive efforts:

Reciprocity: People are generally more willing to comply with requests if they feel they are repaying a favor.

Consistency: People like to be consistent in their behavior. Persuaders can leverage this by getting people to commit, even in a small way, to a position before asking them to commit to something larger.

Social Proof: Individuals are influenced by how they perceive others are thinking or acting. Showing that others agree with or have committed to a position can be persuasive.

Liking: People are more likely to be persuaded by individuals whom they like or find attractive.

Authority: Showing that an idea or behavior is endorsed by an authority figure can increase its persuasive power.

Scarcity: Suggesting that an opportunity is limited can make it more desirable and increase compliance.

Ethical Considerations in Persuasion While persuasion is a powerful tool, it also carries ethical responsibilities. Persuaders must consider the implications of their attempts to influence others. The ethical persuader should:

Respect the autonomy and rights of the audience: Avoid manipulation or coercion, and ensure that persuasion does not infringe on the rights of others.

Be truthful and transparent: Avoid misleading or deceptive tactics.

Promote beneficial outcomes: Use persuasion to promote positive or beneficial changes that enhance the welfare of individuals and the community.

Persuasion is an art that requires understanding human psychology, clear communication, and ethical consideration. By mastering the elements of effective persuasion, individuals can enhance their ability to influence others in both personal and professional contexts. Whether advocating for a cause, selling a product, or navigating personal relationships, effective persuasion and attitude change can lead to significant and meaningful outcomes.

ᗡᗡᗡ

"As we chart the future of social psychology, we must weave the threads of technology and tradition together, crafting approaches that respect our past while preparing us for a digital future."

ᗡᗡᗡ

ELEVEN

THE ROLE OF COMMUNICATION IN SOCIAL INTERACTION

Communication is the backbone of social interaction. It enables individuals to share thoughts, feelings, and information, fostering understanding and connection among people. The role of communication in social interactions is profound, influencing everything from personal relationships to professional environments. This section explores the significance of communication, its various forms, and its impact on social interactions.

Essence and Importance of Communication Communication in social interaction serves multiple functions. It is used to convey information, resolve conflicts, express emotions, build relationships, and influence others. Effective communication is crucial for successful interactions because it helps establish mutual understanding and facilitates collaboration.

Forms of Communication Communication can be verbal, non-verbal, or written, each playing a vital role in social interactions:

Verbal communication involves the use of words to convey messages. This can be done through spoken language or sign language. Clarity, tone, and the choice of words significantly affect how messages are received and interpreted.

Non-verbal communication includes body language, facial expressions, eye contact, gestures, and posture. These cues often convey more about a person's feelings and attitudes than words alone and can either reinforce or contradict what is being said verbally.

Written communication involves expressing ideas in writing. In today's digital age, written communication spans from traditional letters and memos to emails, texts, and social media posts. Each medium has its own norms and expectations that can influence how messages are crafted and understood.

Components of Effective Communication Effective communication involves more than just sending a message; it also requires ensuring the message is received and understood as intended. Key components include:

Clarity and Brevity: Messages should be clear and to the point to avoid misunderstandings.

Active Listening: Good communication requires listening actively to others, not just hearing their words but also understanding the complete message being conveyed.

Feedback: Providing feedback is essential, as it confirms whether a message has been understood correctly and allows for corrections if necessary.

Empathy: Understanding and acknowledging others' feelings and perspectives is crucial in effective communication.

Adaptability: Adjusting communication styles to fit different contexts, situations, and audiences can greatly enhance the effectiveness of the message.

Barriers to Effective Communication Several barriers can impede effective communication, including:

Cultural Differences: Variations in cultural backgrounds can lead to different interpretations of the same message.

Emotional Barriers: Strong emotions such as anger or sadness can prevent a clear understanding of the message being communicated.

Language Barriers: Differences in language or vocabulary can lead to misunderstandings.

Physical Barriers: Noise, distance, or technology issues can obstruct communication.

Perceptual Barriers: Personal biases and stereotypes can distort the understanding of a message.

Communication in Different Social Contexts The role of communication varies across different social contexts:

In Families: Communication is the tool through which family members express care, negotiate space, and resolve conflicts. Effective communication in families builds a foundation of trust.

In Workplaces: In professional settings, communication is key to teamwork, productivity, and leadership. Poor communication can lead to conflicts and decreased productivity, while effective communication can enhance collaboration and efficiency.

In Education: Teachers and students rely on good communication for effective learning. Teachers need to be clear in their instructions and receptive to feedback, while students need to be able to express confusion or curiosity.

In Social Relationships: Communication is essential for building and maintaining friendships and romantic relationships. It helps in sharing personal feelings and thoughts, which is crucial for developing deeper connections.

The role of communication in social interaction is integral and pervasive. Effective communication enhances understanding, builds relationships, resolves conflicts, and improves overall interaction quality. By recognizing the different forms of communication and working to enhance communication skills, individuals can better navigate their social worlds. Understanding and overcoming barriers to effective communication also play a critical role in improving interactions across all areas of life, from personal relationships to professional environments.

ᐳᐳᐳ

"In every queue, every silent adherence to unspoken rules, we see the architecture of society—a structure built on mutual respect and shared understandings."

ϷϷϷ

TWELVE

Conflict and Cooperation: Managing Interpersonal Relations

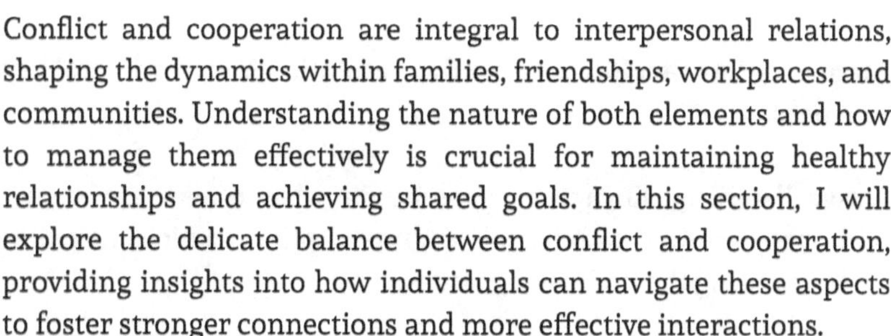

Conflict and cooperation are integral to interpersonal relations, shaping the dynamics within families, friendships, workplaces, and communities. Understanding the nature of both elements and how to manage them effectively is crucial for maintaining healthy relationships and achieving shared goals. In this section, I will explore the delicate balance between conflict and cooperation, providing insights into how individuals can navigate these aspects to foster stronger connections and more effective interactions.

Understanding Conflict Conflict in interpersonal relations arises when there are perceived incompatible goals, needs, desires, or values between individuals or groups. It is a natural part of human interactions and, contrary to common belief, not all conflict is negative. When managed well, conflict can lead to growth, innovation, and strengthened relationships. It can prompt discussion that clarifies misunderstandings and results in solutions that benefit all parties involved.

Sources of Conflict Conflicts can stem from a variety of sources:

Communication breakdowns, where misunderstandings or the lack of open dialogue leads to frustrations.

Differences in values or beliefs, where individuals' core principles clash.

Personality clashes, where differing temperaments lead to regular disagreements.

Resource scarcity, where competition for limited resources, whether material (like money or space) or intangible (like time or attention), creates tension.

Role expectations and responsibilities, where ambiguity or unrealistic expectations regarding roles lead to conflict.

Managing Conflict Effective conflict resolution involves several key practices:

Active listening: Engaging earnestly in what others are saying without planning a rebuttal or interruption, which helps in understanding the underlying issues.

Empathy: Trying to understand the feelings and perspectives of others, which can de-escalate tensions.

Non-confrontational communication: Using "I" statements that express how you feel rather than "you" statements which can sound accusatory.

Seeking common ground: Focusing on areas of agreement before addressing the differences.

Problem-solving orientation: Approaching conflict as a problem to be solved jointly rather than a battle to be won.

Promoting Cooperation While managing conflict is about resolving disagreements, promoting cooperation is about creating an environment where working together is preferred and encouraged. Cooperation is crucial for achieving shared goals and can be significantly rewarding, leading to greater productivity and mutual benefits.

Strategies for Enhancing Cooperation

Establishing clear, shared goals: Ensuring everyone understands and agrees with what the group is trying to achieve.

Building trust: Trust is fundamental for cooperation. It can be built over time through consistent and reliable actions.

Encouraging open communication: Creating channels for open and honest communication where concerns and ideas can be freely shared.

Recognizing contributions: Acknowledging and appreciating each individual's contributions can reinforce cooperative behavior.

Fostering a collaborative environment: Encouraging teamwork and collaborative problem-solving activities can strengthen bonds and promote a cooperative spirit.

Balancing Conflict and Cooperation In any relationship or group setting, there needs to be a healthy balance between managing conflict and fostering cooperation. Too much conflict can lead to a toxic environment, while excessive suppression of conflict to maintain peace can prevent the airing of valid concerns and hinder decision-making processes. Similarly, while cooperation is generally positive, overemphasis on consensus can lead to groupthink, where the desire for harmony overrides realistic appraisal of alternatives.

Practical Applications

In the workplace, understanding and balancing conflict and cooperation can lead to a more productive environment. Managers and team leaders can play pivotal roles by setting the tone for how conflict is handled and how cooperation is rewarded.

In personal relationships, such as with family or friends, managing conflict with empathy and fostering cooperation can enhance bonds and ensure long-term relationships remain strong.

Conflict and cooperation are not mutually exclusive but are interdependent aspects of interpersonal relations. Effectively managing both is key to successful social interactions and the cultivation of environments where individuals can thrive together. By embracing conflict as an opportunity for improvement and promoting cooperation as a standard practice, individuals and groups can enhance their dynamics, leading to more fulfilling and productive relationships.

ϼϼϼ

"Our digital personas are just fragments of our identity, carefully curated and often shielded from the spontaneity of real human interactions."

❦❦❦

THIRTEEN

SOCIAL IDENTITY AND SELF-CONCEPT: WHO WE THINK WE ARE

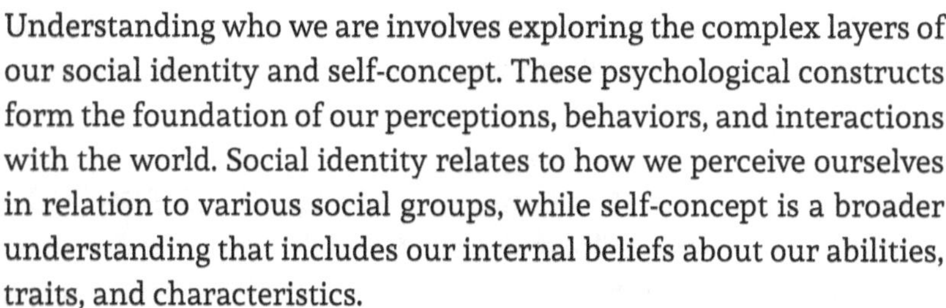

Understanding who we are involves exploring the complex layers of our social identity and self-concept. These psychological constructs form the foundation of our perceptions, behaviors, and interactions with the world. Social identity relates to how we perceive ourselves in relation to various social groups, while self-concept is a broader understanding that includes our internal beliefs about our abilities, traits, and characteristics.

The Concept of Self-Concept Self-concept is essentially how we view ourselves. This view is constructed from our beliefs about who we are, our evaluations of our strengths and weaknesses, and our perceptions of how we fit into the broader social world. It is an all-encompassing framework that includes self-esteem (how much we like or value ourselves) and self-efficacy (our belief in our ability to perform tasks).

Self-concept is shaped by various factors, including familial influences, peer interactions, and societal expectations. For instance, positive reinforcement from parents and teachers can bolster a child's self-esteem, while achievements in academics or sports can enhance self-efficacy. Over time, these experiences amalgamate into a complex set of self-beliefs that guide our thoughts, actions, and reactions.

Understanding Social Identity Social identity theory, developed by Henri Tajfel and John Turner, posits that part of an individual's concept of self comes from the groups to which they belong. This could include groups based on religion, race, gender, profession, and hobbies, among others. Identifying with these groups can significantly influence our behavior and how we interact with others.

Social identity contributes to in-group/out-group dynamics, where individuals tend to favor members of their own group (in-group) over those who are not (out-group). This preference can affect everything from whom we socialize with to how we compete and collaborate, leading to phenomena such as group bias and even discrimination.

Interplay Between Self-Concept and Social Identity The relationship between self-concept and social identity is dynamic. While our group memberships help form part of our self-concept, our self-perception can also influence which groups we choose to join or identify with.

This interplay can be particularly evident in adolescence and young adulthood, where identity exploration is prominent.

For instance, a teenager might develop a part of their self-concept around being an athlete. This aspect of their identity influences not only how they see themselves but also the social groups they interact with, such as fellow athletes. Conversely, their self-concept might change if they no longer identify with this group or if they join a different group where different qualities are valued, such as an academic club.

Effects on Behavior and Interactions The way we understand ourselves and our social identities impacts our behavior in several ways. For example, a strong, positive self-concept can lead to better mental health, higher resilience, and more effective coping strategies in stressful situations.

On the other hand, a fragmented or negative self-concept might contribute to emotional and psychological difficulties such as anxiety and depression.

In social interactions, our identities can dictate the roles we assume. Individuals who perceive themselves as leaders may naturally take charge in group settings, influencing group decisions and dynamics. Similarly, those who see themselves as caretakers might predominantly engage in supportive roles within their personal and professional relationships.

Challenges and Growth The development of self-concept and social identity is not always linear or positive. Experiences of failure, rejection, or discrimination can negatively impact how we view ourselves. However, such challenges also provide opportunities for growth. Engaging in self-reflection, seeking feedback from trusted peers, and exploring new roles or groups can lead to a more integrated and flexible self-concept.

Social identity and self-concept are foundational to understanding ourselves and navigating the social world. They influence our thoughts, behaviors, and interactions, shaping how we connect with others and move through society.

By continuously engaging with and refining our self-concept and understanding our social identities, we can lead more fulfilled and effective lives, marked by better relationships and a clearer sense of self.

❧❧❧

"The greatest challenge of modern social interactions is to remain genuine in a world that often rewards the superficial."

❧❧❧

FOURTEEN

PREJUDICE AND INTERGROUP RELATIONS: OVERCOMING BARRIERS

Prejudice and its impact on intergroup relations continue to be significant issues in contemporary society. These social phenomena affect how groups interact, influencing personal behaviors and societal outcomes. Let's understand the nature of prejudice, its origins, its effects on intergroup relations, and the strategies to overcome these barriers to foster more inclusive and harmonious social environments.

Understanding Prejudice Prejudice is a preconceived opinion that is not based on reason or actual experience; it is a bias that can be positive but is more often negative. While individuals may believe their biases are grounded in rational thought, prejudices are typically rooted in stereotypes and unfounded beliefs rather than factual or personal experiences. These prejudiced attitudes can lead to discriminatory behaviors, where individuals or groups are treated unfairly based on their perceived group membership rather than their individual qualities or actions.

Origins of Prejudice The origins of prejudice are multifaceted, involving psychological, social, and cultural elements. Psychologically, prejudice can stem from the human tendency to categorize the world, including other people, to simplify information processing. This categorization process often leads to us-versus-them thinking, where individuals define in-groups (groups they belong to) and out-groups (groups they do not belong to).

Socially, prejudices are often passed down through generations within a culture or community, embedded in the norms and values taught to children from a young age. Culturally, media portrayals, historical narratives, and national rhetoric can reinforce stereotypes and biased perceptions about different groups.

Effects on Intergroup Relations Prejudice can severely impact intergroup relations, leading to mistrust, avoidance, and conflict. In the workplace, prejudice can result in unfair hiring practices, limited opportunities for advancement for certain groups, and a hostile work environment. In educational settings, biases can affect how students interact with each other and influence teacher expectations and student performance. On a broader societal level, prejudice can lead to systemic inequalities and social divisions that affect every aspect of individuals' lives, including access to healthcare, education, and justice.

Overcoming Prejudice and Improving Intergroup Relations To overcome prejudice and improve intergroup relations, a multifaceted approach is necessary. This approach can involve individual actions, institutional policies, and societal changes:

Education and Awareness: Educating people about the origins and consequences of prejudice and exposing them to information that contradicts their stereotypes can reduce prejudiced beliefs. Programs that focus on multicultural education, diversity training, and inclusive curriculums can help cultivate a more understanding and accepting society.

Intergroup Contact: Encouraging direct interaction between members of different groups can reduce prejudice. This is based on the contact hypothesis, which posits that under appropriate conditions, interpersonal contact is one of the most effective ways to reduce prejudice between majority and minority group members. These interactions can help individuals see each other more as unique individuals and less as faceless members of an out-group.

Empathy Development: Fostering empathy through perspective-taking exercises can decrease bias. When individuals are able to place themselves in another's situation, they are more likely to recognize injustices and reconsider their own prejudiced attitudes.

Institutional Support: Organizations and governments can play a critical role by enacting and enforcing policies that promote fairness and equality. This includes anti-discrimination laws, equitable hiring practices, and support for affirmative action programs.

Community and Dialogue: Building communities that encourage dialogue and interaction among diverse groups can facilitate understanding and cooperation. Community programs, intergroup dialogues, and joint community projects can bring people together to work on common goals and reduce perceptions of difference.

Media Representation: Promoting positive and diverse representations of different groups in the media can help change perceptions and reduce stereotypes. This involves supporting media outlets and programming that provide balanced and fair portrayals of various groups.

Prejudice and poor intergroup relations pose significant barriers to social cohesion and collective progress. By understanding the roots of these issues and actively engaging in strategies to address them, individuals and societies can move towards more inclusive, fair, and harmonious interactions. Overcoming prejudice requires continuous effort and commitment at all levels of society—from individual self-reflection and education to systemic changes in how institutions operate. Through these efforts, it is possible to break down barriers and build a more equitable world.

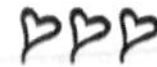

"Empathy is the quiet force that can dissolve cultural barriers, illuminate shared values, and foster understanding across diverse communities."

▷▷▷

FIFTEEN

HELPING AND ALTRUISM: THE GOOD IN US

Helping behavior and altruism are aspects of human nature that reveal our capacity for kindness and selflessness. Understanding why and how we help others not only sheds light on the positive aspects of human behavior but also promotes a more cooperative and compassionate society. Here we will learn the psychological underpinnings of helping and altruism, the benefits of such behaviors, and the factors that can enhance or inhibit our inclination to help others.

The Nature of Helping and Altruism Helping behavior refers to voluntary actions intended to aid others with no expectation of reward. Altruism, a form of helping behavior, involves selfless concern for the well-being of others, even at a cost to oneself. While helping might be motivated by anticipated gain, such as a return favor, social approval, or a boost in self-esteem, altruism is purely motivated by the desire to benefit someone else.

Why We Help: Psychological Perspectives Several theories explain why people engage in helping behaviors:

Evolutionary Theory suggests that helping behavior evolved because it increased the chances of survival for our ancestors. Behaviors like sharing food, caring for the young, and protecting each other from threats enhanced group survival and were passed down through generations.

Social Exchange Theory posits that people help others based on a cost-benefit analysis. If the perceived benefits of helping outweigh the costs, people are more likely to act. Benefits might not always be material; they can include psychological rewards like feeling good about oneself.

Empathy-Altruism Hypothesis argues that empathic concern for others can motivate altruistic behavior. When we empathize with someone, we are more likely to help them, regardless of what we might gain from the action.

Factors Influencing Helping Behavior Several factors can influence whether and how people engage in helping behaviors:

Empathy: Feeling empathy for another person is a strong motivator for altruistic actions. The ability to understand and share the feelings of another person can prompt us to act in their interest.

Mood: People are more likely to help others when they are in a good mood. Positive emotions increase generosity and reduce the perceived costs of helping.

Social Norms: Cultural and social norms can greatly influence helping behavior. Norms such as the norm of reciprocity (helping others who have helped us) and the norm of social responsibility (helping those who need assistance) guide social conduct.

Responsibility: People are more likely to help if they feel a personal responsibility to act. If others are present, the sense of responsibility might be diffused among the group, a phenomenon known as the bystander effect.

The Benefits of Helping Helping others can have several benefits for both the giver and the receiver:

Psychological Well-Being: Engaging in helping behaviors can enhance the helper's mood and self-esteem. Acts of kindness release endorphins, producing the so-called "helper's high."

Social Benefits: Helping can strengthen social bonds and foster positive social interactions. Altruistic communities tend to be more cohesive and safer places to live.

Reciprocal Help: Societies that encourage helping behavior may benefit from a more supportive social environment where people feel more secure in knowing that others will help them in times of need.

Promoting Altruism and Helping Behaviors Promoting helping behaviors and altruism involves creating environments that encourage such acts:

Education and Awareness: Teaching empathy and social responsibility from a young age can cultivate a culture of helping. Educational programs that include service learning or community service can integrate these values into daily practice.

Modeling and Reinforcement: Positive reinforcement of helping behaviors and public recognition of altruistic acts can motivate others to act similarly. Additionally, seeing others engage in helping behaviors can serve as a powerful model for individuals.

Reducing Barriers: Making it easier for people to help by reducing logistical, financial, or emotional barriers can increase helping behaviors. For example, organizing community events where people can volunteer in accessible ways encourages participation.

Conclusion Understanding the psychological foundations of helping and altruism illuminates a vital aspect of human behavior. By fostering environments that encourage these behaviors and understanding the factors that enhance or inhibit our propensity to help, we can nurture the good in us and build more supportive, empathetic, and cooperative communities. In doing so, we not only improve the lives of others but also enrich our own lives through the profound satisfaction that comes from genuine acts of kindness.

"In the theatre of social dynamics, roles are not just played; they are lived, shaping how we see ourselves and how others perceive us."

ᐅᐅᐅ

SIXTEEN

THE IMPACT OF SOCIAL MEDIA: CONNECTIONS AND ISOLATIONS

Social media has become an integral part of modern life, profoundly influencing how we communicate, interact, and perceive the world around us. While it offers unprecedented opportunities for connecting with others, it also presents unique challenges, including potential feelings of isolation and loneliness.

Connecting Through Social Media Social media platforms like Facebook, Twitter, Instagram, and LinkedIn are designed to foster connections by allowing users to share updates, interests, and experiences. These platforms provide several significant benefits:

Global Connectivity: Social media breaks down geographical barriers, enabling people to connect with others across the globe. This connectivity allows for the sharing of ideas, cultures, and perspectives, enriching users' experiences and understanding of the world.

Community Building: Many users find communities of like-minded individuals on social media. Whether through groups focused on hobbies, support networks, or professional associations, these communities provide a sense of belonging and identity.

Information Access: Social media is a powerful tool for the dissemination of information. Users can receive updates on current events, learn about new topics, and access educational resources that may not be available locally.

Support and Solidarity: During crises or significant global events, social media can be a platform for solidarity and support. Fundraising, awareness campaigns, and community support initiatives often find traction on these platforms.

The Isolating Effects of Social Media Despite its benefits, social media can also contribute to feelings of isolation and loneliness for several reasons:

Superficial Connections: While social media enables increased connectivity, the quality of these connections is often questioned. Interactions on social media can sometimes be superficial, lacking the depth and emotional support that face-to-face interactions provide.

Social Comparison: Social media platforms are rife with opportunities for social comparison, as users often post highlights of their lives that may not represent everyday reality. This can lead to feelings of inadequacy, envy, and decreased self-esteem among other users, who may feel their lives do not measure up.

Overwhelm and Anxiety: The sheer volume of content and the pressure to be constantly available and responsive on social media can lead to overwhelm and anxiety. The "fear of missing out," or

FOMO, is a phenomenon linked to intense social media use, where users feel an obligation to stay continually connected so they do not miss anything.

Cyberbullying and Trolling: Social media can also be a platform for negative interactions, including bullying and harassment. The anonymity and distance provided by the internet can embolden individuals to engage in harmful behaviors that they might not exhibit in person.

Navigating Social Media for Healthy Connections To harness the benefits of social media while minimizing its negative effects, users can adopt several strategies:

Mindful Usage: Being mindful of the time spent on social media and the purpose of usage can help mitigate adverse effects. Users can benefit from setting specific times for social media use and taking regular breaks.

Quality Over Quantity: Focusing on cultivating deeper, more meaningful connections rather than acquiring numerous superficial relationships can enhance the quality of social interactions on these platforms.

Critical Consumption: Developing a critical approach to consuming content on social media can reduce the impact of negative comparisons. Understanding that what people choose to share is often a curated version of their lives can help maintain perspective.

Seeking Face-to-Face Interactions: Balancing online interactions with face-to-face communication can help maintain genuine social connections and support mental health.

Social media is a complex tool with the power to both connect and isolate. Its impact varies significantly among individuals, influenced by how they choose to engage with the technology.

By understanding and addressing the challenges associated with social media use, individuals can enjoy the benefits of global connectivity and community building while mitigating the risks of isolation and anxiety. As we continue to integrate social media into our lives, it is crucial to strive for a balanced approach that fosters genuine human connections and promotes overall well-being.

ᗡᗡᗡ

"The resilience of any community facing environmental challenges hinges not just on resources or policies, but on the social bonds that weave individuals into a cohesive unit."

ﬔﬔﬔ

SEVENTEEN

BEHAVIOR IN PUBLIC SPACES: UNSPOKEN SOCIAL RULES

Behavior in public spaces is governed by a complex set of unspoken social rules that dictate how individuals should act in various settings outside their private lives. These rules, while not legally binding, are crucial for maintaining order and decency in society.

Understanding Unspoken Social Rules Unspoken social rules are the norms that we follow without necessarily being aware of them. These rules can vary significantly from one culture to another but generally include expectations about politeness, personal space, noise levels, and more. For example, it's commonly accepted that one should lower their voice when talking on the phone in a public transport setting or that one should stand in line without pushing ahead of others.

The Importance of Social Norms in Public Spaces Social norms serve several important functions in public spaces:

Facilitating Predictable Interactions: Social norms help make interactions more predictable, reducing uncertainty and making public spaces more navigable. For example, pedestrian traffic rules suggest walking on a specific side of the pathway to avoid collisions.

Promoting Order and Efficiency: In places like subway systems and airports, efficiency is key to functionality. Social norms help in managing large crowds, ensuring that people move smoothly and efficiently.

Enhancing Safety: Many social norms are in place to ensure safety. For example, driving on a designated side of the road or following signs and signals helps prevent accidents.

Fostering Respectful and Considerate Behavior: Social norms often promote behaviors that are considerate of others. This includes keeping public spaces clean, not using offensive language, and respecting others' privacy and space.

Examples of Unspoken Social Rules Several examples illustrate how unspoken rules govern our behavior in public spaces:

Queueing: Virtually anywhere in the world, forming a line and waiting your turn is a respected practice. Skipping the line is generally frowned upon and can lead to public disapproval.

Tipping: In many cultures, tipping service providers is an expected practice, which is seen as a way to show appreciation for the service rendered.

Dress Codes: Certain public spaces like churches, fine dining restaurants, and private clubs often have unspoken dress codes that visitors are expected to follow.

Cell Phone Usage: There is an increasing emphasis on minimizing cell phone usage in certain public contexts, such as during theater performances or in quiet compartments of trains.

The Consequences of Not Following Social Norms Failing to adhere to these unspoken rules can lead to various negative outcomes:

Social Sanctions: Individuals who break social norms might face informal sanctions such as disapproval, judgment, or being publicly called out.

Isolation and Rejection: Repeated failure to comply with social norms can lead to social isolation, where individuals find themselves excluded from social groups because they are seen as uncooperative or disrespectful.

Missed Opportunities: Professional and social opportunities may be lost if individuals consistently fail to adhere to the expected norms, particularly in formal settings.

Navigating Unspoken Rules Navigating these unspoken rules requires a keen observation and adaptability:

Cultural Sensitivity: When entering a new cultural context, it is important to observe and adapt to the local norms to avoid misunderstandings.

Learning from Observation: Watching how others behave in specific settings can provide valuable clues about what is expected.

Asking for Clarification: If unsure, asking a local or a peer for clarification can help avoid faux pas.

The unspoken social rules that govern behavior in public spaces play a crucial role in maintaining societal order and ensuring that public interactions are conducted smoothly and respectfully. While these rules can vary widely across different cultures and settings, their overarching goal is to promote harmony and efficiency. By understanding and adhering to these norms, individuals contribute to a more respectful and functional society. Understanding these rules is not just about following the crowd but about fostering an environment where everyone can coexist peacefully and productively.

ϸϸϸ

"Social norms are not just passive practices; they are active affirmations of a community's values and expectations."

⮞⮞⮞

EIGHTEEN

Coping with Social Anxiety: Strategies and Insights

Social anxiety is a common condition that affects millions of people worldwide, characterized by an intense fear of social situations that can lead to avoidance and significant distress. Understanding and managing social anxiety is crucial for those affected to lead fulfilling and engaging lives.

Understanding Social Anxiety Social anxiety disorder, also known as social phobia, involves an excessive and unreasonable fear of social situations. Individuals with this condition fear being judged, embarrassed, or criticized by others. This fear can be so overwhelming that it interferes with work, school, and other everyday activities, and can prevent the formation or maintenance of social relationships.

Symptoms of Social Anxiety Symptoms of social anxiety can vary widely but typically include intense nervousness and discomfort in social situations, racing heart, excessive sweating, trembling, a strong desire to avoid social interactions, and sometimes panic attacks. The anticipation of a social situation can often be as debilitating as the actual event.

Cognitive-Behavioral Strategies for Managing Social Anxiety One of the most effective treatments for social anxiety is cognitive-behavioral therapy (CBT). This approach involves identifying and challenging negative thoughts and gradually confronting feared social situations:

Cognitive Restructuring: This technique helps individuals identify and challenge unhelpful, often distorted thoughts that contribute to social anxiety. By examining these thoughts critically, individuals can begin to replace them with more realistic and positive ones.

Exposure Therapy: Gradual exposure to feared social situations is another key component of CBT. Starting with less intimidating interactions and progressively moving to more challenging scenarios can help reduce anxiety through repeated experiences and desensitization.

Skill Training: For some, social anxiety stems from a lack of confidence in social skills. Practicing these skills, such as starting conversations, making eye contact, and expressing opinions, can improve competence and confidence in social settings.

Behavioral Techniques Several behavioral techniques can also help manage symptoms of social anxiety:

Relaxation Techniques: Methods such as deep breathing, progressive muscle relaxation, and mindfulness meditation can help control the physical symptoms of anxiety.

Visualization: Imagining oneself successfully navigating a social situation can help build confidence and reduce anxiety. This technique involves vividly picturing a successful interaction and mentally rehearsing before facing the situation in reality.

Lifestyle Adjustments: Regular exercise, adequate sleep, and a healthy diet can improve overall mental health and help reduce symptoms of anxiety. Avoiding excessive caffeine and alcohol can also be beneficial, as these can exacerbate anxiety symptoms.

Social Support and Therapy Building a supportive network is vital for individuals struggling with social anxiety. This can involve:

Seeking Professional Help: Engaging with a therapist who specializes in anxiety disorders can provide guidance and support. Therapy can be a safe space to explore the roots of social anxiety and develop strategies to overcome it.

Support Groups: Joining a support group where members share similar experiences and challenges can provide a sense of belonging and an opportunity to practice social skills in a non-judgmental environment.

Educating Friends and Family: Informing loved ones about social anxiety can help them understand the condition better, enabling them to provide support and accommodate needs during social interactions.

Practical Daily Tips In addition to structured therapy and support, there are practical daily tips that can help manage social anxiety:

Setting Small Goals: Breaking social challenges into smaller, manageable goals can make them less daunting. For example, if attending a party feels overwhelming, one might aim to stay for just 30 minutes or speak to at least two people.

Keeping a Journal: Writing about social experiences and feelings can help track progress and clarify thoughts and anxieties, making them easier to address with a therapist or support group.

Practicing Assertiveness: Learning to express oneself assertively rather than passively or aggressively can improve interactions and reduce feelings of anxiety and helplessness.

Coping with social anxiety involves a combination of understanding the psychological aspects of the disorder, employing cognitive-behavioral techniques, seeking support, and making practical daily adjustments. While overcoming social anxiety can be challenging, with the right strategies and support, individuals can enhance their ability to interact with others and participate more fully in life. The journey to overcoming social anxiety is gradual, and celebrating small victories along the way can be incredibly empowering.

ᗡᗡᗡ

"As the lines between work and life blur in our digital age, maintaining a balance between connectivity and personal space becomes crucial."

❦❦❦

NINETEEN

SOCIAL PSYCHOLOGY IN THE WORKPLACE: COLLABORATION AND COMPETITION

The workplace is a complex environment where the principles of social psychology are vividly manifested through collaboration and competition. Understanding how these dynamics operate can significantly enhance organizational effectiveness and employee satisfaction.

The Role of Collaboration in the Workplace Collaboration in the workplace refers to the efforts of multiple individuals working together to achieve a common goal. This cooperative spirit is crucial for the success of any organization as it leads to the sharing of ideas, pooling of resources, and synergy that often results in increased creativity and productivity.

Psychological Foundations of Collaboration: Collaboration is underpinned by several psychological principles, including social facilitation, where the presence of others positively impacts performance. Additionally, the concept of social loafing, which suggests that individuals may exert less effort in a group compared to working alone, is an important consideration. Effective collaboration requires strategies to mitigate social loafing by ensuring clear individual accountability within the group.

Benefits of Effective Collaboration: When collaboration is well-executed, it can lead to enhanced problem-solving capabilities and innovation. Diverse teams that bring together varied perspectives and expertise are particularly effective at tackling complex problems. Moreover, collaboration can improve job satisfaction and employee retention, as workers feel more engaged and appreciated in their roles.

Understanding Competition in the Workplace While collaboration focuses on jointly achieving goals, competition involves a scenario where individuals or groups vie to achieve a goal that cannot be shared. In the workplace, competition can be a double-edged sword.

Positive Aspects of Competition: Healthy competition can be a potent motivator, pushing individuals to improve their performance and efficiency. It can drive innovation and excellence by encouraging employees to outdo their past performances and set higher standards for their work.

Negative Aspects of Competition: On the flip side, excessive competition can lead to stress, decreased teamwork, and unethical behavior as individuals may prioritize winning or achieving targets at the expense of collaboration and organizational harmony.

Balancing Collaboration and Competition Balancing these two elements is crucial for any organization aiming to harness the benefits of both without falling into potential pitfalls.

Creating a Supportive Culture: Organizations can foster a culture that promotes both healthy competition and robust collaboration. This involves setting clear expectations about the importance of ethical behavior and teamwork, even in competitive scenarios.

Structured Competition: Implementing structured competitive strategies that reward group achievements as well as individual efforts can help maintain balance. For example, team-based competitions or recognition programs that reward not only the results but also the collaborative efforts behind them can be effective.

Conflict Management: Given that both competition and collaboration can lead to conflicts, effective conflict management strategies are essential. Training employees in conflict resolution skills and maintaining open channels of communication are critical.

Reward Systems: Developing reward systems that acknowledge both individual achievements and team contributions can encourage a healthy balance between working together and working against each other. This might include bonuses for individual sales targets as well as team-based project completions.

Social Identity and Team Dynamics The concept of social identity plays a significant role in how collaborative and competitive dynamics unfold in the workplace. Employees often identify with their smaller working groups or departments, and this can influence their behavior and interactions with others.

Enhancing Group Identity: Strengthening a collective group identity can enhance collaboration by reducing in-group and out-group biases. Initiatives that foster a sense of belonging to the organization as a whole, such as company-wide events or internal communications that emphasize shared goals and values, can mitigate divisions.

Understanding the social psychology behind collaboration and competition is vital for any workplace aiming to enhance both employee satisfaction and organizational performance. By fostering an environment where collaboration is encouraged and competition is kept healthy and structured, companies can create a dynamic workplace where innovation and productivity thrive. Ultimately, the key lies in recognizing the strengths and limitations of each approach and strategically implementing practices that capitalize on their benefits while minimizing their drawbacks.

ᗞᗞᗞ

"In the push and pull of social interactions, the art
of persuasion is not about dominance but about
finding and aligning with common ground."

ppp

TWENTY

FUTURE TRENDS IN SOCIAL PSYCHOLOGY: WHERE DO WE GO FROM HERE?

Social psychology has always been a dynamic field, evolving with societal changes and technological advancements. As we look to the future, several emerging trends are poised to shape the direction of social psychology, influencing both theoretical developments and practical applications.

Technological Advancements and Social Media One of the most significant influences on social psychology in the future will likely be continued technological advancements, particularly in the realm of social media and artificial intelligence (AI). Social media has already transformed how people interact, form relationships, and maintain social norms. As these platforms evolve, social psychologists will increasingly focus on understanding the implications of digital interactions on self-esteem, identity, and interpersonal relationships. Moreover, AI and machine learning offer new tools for analyzing vast amounts of data on human behavior, providing deeper insights into complex social interactions.

Virtual Reality and Augmented Reality: Technologies like virtual reality (VR) and augmented reality (AR) are starting to be used in psychological research and therapy. These tools can create simulated environments that allow for the safe exploration of phobias, social interactions, and more, offering controlled settings for experiments that were previously impossible.

Globalization and Cultural Exchange As the world becomes more interconnected, the study of cross-cultural interactions and multiculturalism will become even more critical. Social psychologists will likely focus more on understanding how cultural contexts influence social behaviors and how individuals from different backgrounds negotiate their cultural identities. This research will be crucial for addressing global challenges such as immigration, integration, and international collaboration.

Cultural Competence: There will be an increased emphasis on cultural competence—understanding and respecting differences among cultures. This knowledge will be crucial not just for academics and clinicians but for anyone operating in a globalized workplace or society.

Climate Change and Environmental Issues The role of social psychology in understanding and addressing environmental challenges is another area poised for growth. As the effects of climate change become more apparent, social psychologists are increasingly tasked with understanding the psychological barriers to environmental action and developing strategies to promote sustainable behavior.

Community and Resilience: Research will likely focus on how communities can foster resilience and adapt to environmental changes. This includes studying how social norms and behaviors can evolve to support sustainability initiatives.

Health and Well-being The integration of social psychology with health sciences is expected to deepen. Understanding the social determinants of health, including how socioeconomic status, community support, and cultural factors influence health behaviors, is vital for developing effective public health interventions.

Behavioral Health Interventions: Social psychology will continue to inform the development of behavioral health interventions that address issues from smoking cessation to mental health and obesity. These interventions will increasingly consider social and cultural factors to enhance their effectiveness.

Ethical Considerations and Policy Impact As social psychology continues to influence various aspects of society, ethical considerations will become even more critical. The application of social psychological research in policy-making, business, and technology will require careful consideration of privacy, consent, and potential biases.

Influence on Public Policy: Social psychologists will likely play a more prominent role in shaping public policies related to social issues such as discrimination, education, and healthcare. Their expertise will be crucial in designing policies that are informed by an understanding of human behavior.

The future of social psychology promises expanded opportunities for research and greater integration into various sectors of society. As the field adapts to new technologies, global challenges, and societal shifts, its insights will be crucial for understanding and improving the human condition. By embracing interdisciplinary approaches and prioritizing ethical considerations, social psychology can make significant contributions to a range of important areas—from enhancing individual well-being to tackling global issues. As we look forward, the continued evolution of social psychology will be vital for helping society navigate the complexities of human behavior in an increasingly interconnected world.

ᗡᗡᗡ

"Addressing social anxiety isn't just about
individual strategies; it's about cultivating
environments that acknowledge and adapt to this
widespread challenge."

ᖇᖇᖇ

TWENTY-ONE

SUMMARY

This book is an insightful exploration of how social psychology illuminates the everyday interactions and relationships that shape our world. This comprehensive book delves into the nuanced ways that individuals connect with one another and how these interactions are influenced by broader social forces. Through a blend of engaging examples, cutting-edge research, and practical applications, the book offers a deep understanding of the often invisible forces that guide human behavior in various contexts.

The book begins by laying the groundwork with a discussion on the basics of social connections. It emphasizes the significance of early relationships and their long-lasting impact on individual behavior, exploring theories such as attachment theory and social identity theory. The text explains how early attachments influence future relational patterns and how individuals perceive themselves within their social groups.

As the book progresses, it explores the complex nature of human interactions through the lens of various social psychological theories. For instance, it examines the science of first impressions and their enduring impact on social relationships. The narrative explains how quick judgments based on minimal information can set the tone for future interactions and relationships, highlighting the importance of non-verbal cues like body language and facial expressions in these initial encounters.

Further, the book delves into the formation of friendships and romantic relationships, explaining the roles of similarity, proximity, and reciprocity in developing meaningful connections. It discusses how mutual understanding and shared experiences are central to forming close bonds and how these relationships evolve over time.

In discussing group dynamics, the book sheds light on the roles individuals play within groups and the impact of these roles on group behavior. It addresses how group identities influence personal behavior and how groups manage conflict and cooperation. The text also explores the delicate balance between individuality and group conformity, highlighting the social norms that regulate behavior in group settings.

Leadership and power dynamics within groups receive significant attention, with discussions on how different leadership styles affect group outcomes and the complex interplay between power, influence, and group dynamics. The book illustrates how effective leadership fosters a positive environment and how power can be used responsibly to motivate and guide others.

One of the pivotal themes in the book is the role of communication in social interactions. It underscores the importance of effective communication in building and maintaining relationships, resolving conflicts, and promoting understanding. The book provides practical advice on improving communication skills, such as active listening and empathy.

The book also tackles the influence of social media on human connections, discussing both the opportunities and challenges it presents. It examines how social media has transformed the way people connect, share information, and maintain relationships, while also considering the potential for isolation and miscommunication in digital spaces.

Addressing prejudices and intergroup relations, the book provides insights into overcoming social biases and enhancing interactions among diverse groups. It offers strategies for reducing prejudice and promoting inclusivity through education, exposure, and empathy.

In its concluding chapters, the book discusses future trends in social psychology, particularly focusing on the implications of technological advancements and globalization on human interactions. It speculates on how emerging technologies like artificial intelligence and virtual reality will shape human behavior and social norms in the coming years.

Throughout, this book offers a rich examination of the intricate ways in which our social environments influence our thoughts, feelings, and behaviors. It combines theoretical depth with practical insights, making it a valuable resource for understanding and improving the social dynamics that shape our everyday lives.

ৡৡৡ

Citation And References

This book represents the culmination of extensive research and meticulous analysis, incorporating a diverse range of sources, including numerous books, scholarly studies, and personal experiences. Additionally, I have scoured various websites to gather relevant information and data essential for the compilation of this work. I have taken every precaution to ensure the accuracy of the information presented and have diligently cited all sources to acknowledge their contributions.

Despite these efforts, the possibility of inadvertent errors remains. I deeply value the insights of my readers and appreciate any feedback that can help identify and rectify such inaccuracies. I encourage you to bring any discrepancies to my attention.

Your feedback is not only welcome but crucial, as it will aid in correcting current editions and enhancing the content of future ones. I am committed to maintaining the highest standards of accuracy and reliability in my work and thank you for your support and understanding.

Additionally, I firmly uphold the principle of freedom of speech and expression as guaranteed under Article 19(1)(a) of the Constitution of India, and I respect the diverse viewpoints and expressions of all readers.

ppp

Other Books Of The Author

1. Empowering Minds: A Journey into Women's Self-Discovery and Power
2. The Dynamics of Motivation: Catalyzing Thought into Action
3. Meditation and Mental Well Being: The Path to Inner Peace and Clarity
4. The Psychology of Child Education: Nurturing Future Generations
5. Ethical Enlightenment: A Modern Guide to Living with Integrity
6. Voices of Empowerment: Stories of Women Rising Against Odds
7. Social Psychology in Everyday Life: Understanding Human Connections
8. The Essence of Motivational Speaking: Inspiring Change in Others
9. Balancing Acts: Women, Work, and the Will to Lead
10. Mindful Parenting: Raising Children with Compassion and Awareness
11. The Power of Positive Aging: Embracing Life After Fifty
12. Building Resilient Communities: Social Work in Action
13. The Ethical Educator: Principles for Teaching and Learning
14. From Insight to Impact: Social Psychology for a Better World
15. Cultivating Compassion: A Guide to Ethical Living
16. The Science of Self-Help: Navigating Life's Challenges with Psychological Wisdom
17. The Mindful Leader: Meditation Techniques for Modern Management
18. Breaking Barriers: Women's Pathways to Leadership and Empowerment
19. Educating Hearts: The Role of Emotional Intelligence in Child Development
20. Transformative Talks: Insights into Motivational Oratory
21. Green Ethics: A Path to Sustainable Living

ppp

Contact

Dr. Minakshi Bansal
Social Activist
Ahmedabad, Gujarat, Bharat
minakshiindiag20@yahoo.com

❦❦❦

|| LOKAHA SAMASTHAHA SUKHINO BHAVANTU ||